I Know That!

animals

ewellyn

W

FRANKLIN WATTS

LONDON • SYDNEY

First published in 2003
by Franklin Watts
338 Euston Road
London NW1 3BH

Franklin Watts Australia
Level 17/207 Kent Street
Sydney NSW 2000

Text copyright © Claire Llewellyn 2003
Design and concept © Franklin Watts 2003

Educational advisor: Gill Matthews, non-fiction literacy
  consultant and Inset trainer
Editor: Rachel Cooke
Designer: James Marks
Acknowledgements: J C Allen/FLPA: 19. Ian Beames/Ecoscene: 21. Frank Blackburn/Ecoscene: 20. Andrew Brown/
Ecoscene: 8. Mark Edwards/Still Pictures: 4, 22c. Eye Ubiquitous: 11. Pierre Gleizes/Still Pictures: 9. Paul Glendell/
Still Pictures: 13b. Chinch Gryniewicz/Ecoscene: 12, 22b. Angela Hampton/Ecoscene: 1, 2, 5, 14b, 16. Anthony
Harrison/Ecoscene: 10. Hubert Klein/Still Pictures: 15. Joy Michaud/Ecoscene: front cover, 6. Thomas Raupach/Still
Pictures: 7b. Roland Seitre/Still Pictures: 18, 23cr. David Wootton/Ecoscene: 17, 23bl. Harry Cory-Wright: 14c, 23tl.

A CIP catalogue record for this book is available from the British Library

ISBN: 978 0 7496 8123 4

Printed in Malaysia

Franklin Watts is a division of Hachette Children's Books, an Hachette Livre UK company.

Contents

Living on a farm

Many animals live on farms.
Farmers give animals food and shelter.

Farmers help animals care for their babies.

There are farms all over the country. Some of them are even in towns. Where is your nearest farm?

A herd of cows

Many farmers keep cows.
Cows give us milk and meat.

▲ *A calf drinks milk from its mother.*

Farmers milk cows twice a day.

How much milk do you drink? Milk from cows is used to make yogurt, butter and cheese. Do you eat yogurt, butter and cheese?

Field or shed?

For most of the year, cows live in fields. In winter, they are kept in sheds.

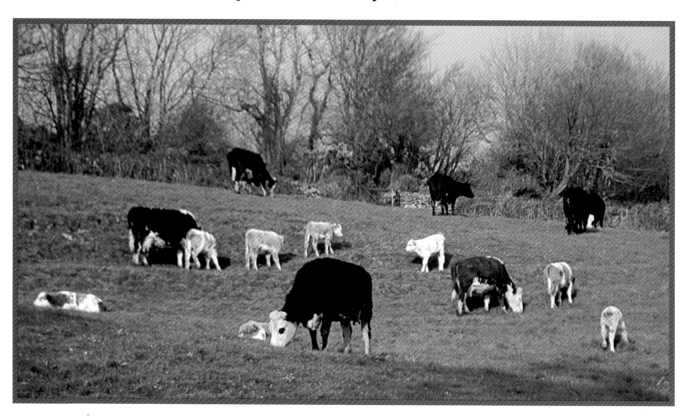

▲ *In the field, cows graze on grass.*

In the shed, the farmer gives the cows their food.

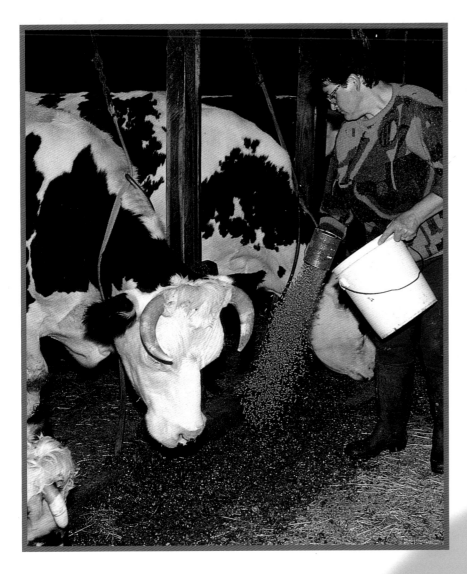

A cow is
a female animal.
The male is
called a bull.
A cow's baby is
called a calf.
We call all these
animals 'cattle'.

A flock of sheep

Many farmers keep sheep. Sheep give us wool, meat and milk.

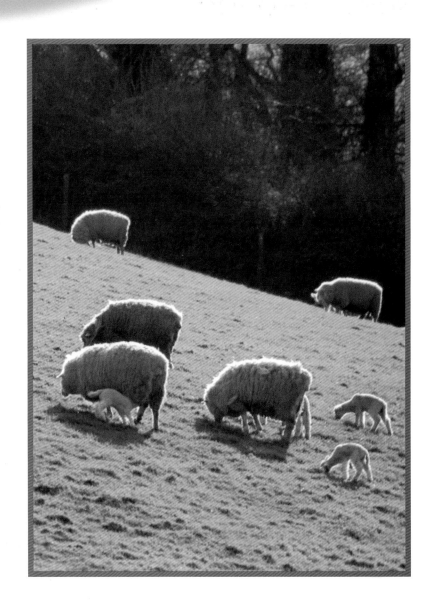

▶ *Sheep have one or two lambs in the spring.*

A sheepdog helps to move sheep around the farm.

A female sheep is called a ewe. A male sheep is called a ram. A baby sheep is called a lamb.

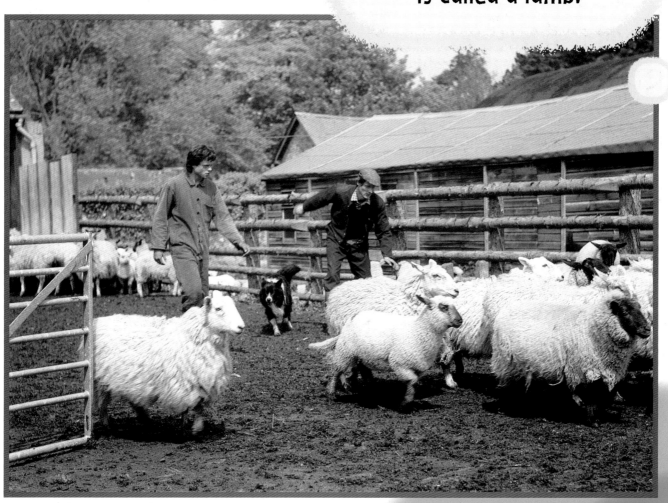

A warm coat

Sheep have a woolly coat that keeps them warm.

▼ *Sheep can live outside all year round.*

A sheep's coat is cut every year.

We use sheep's wool to make clothes like jumpers, hats, scarves and gloves. What do woollen things feel like?

Keeping chickens

Some farmers keep chickens. They give us eggs and meat.

Chickens' eggs are good to eat.

Some chickens are kept outside.

A female chicken is called a hen. The male is called a cock. A baby is called a chick.

◀ *Some chickens are kept in cages.*

Keeping pigs

Some farmers keep pigs. They give us meat such as bacon and ham.

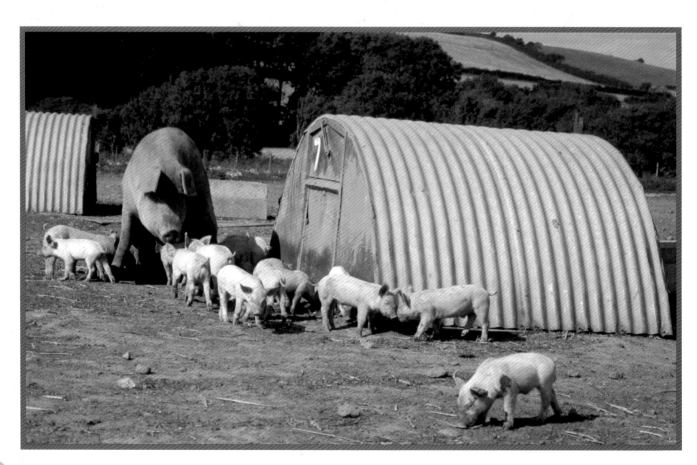

A female pig is called a sow. The male is called a boar. A baby pig is called a piglet.

Most pigs are kept inside.

Some pigs live outside. They shelter in pigsties.

Other farm animals

Other animals live on farms.
They help the farmer in
different ways.

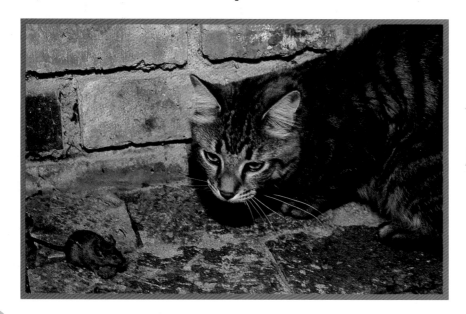

*Cats catch
mice and rats.*

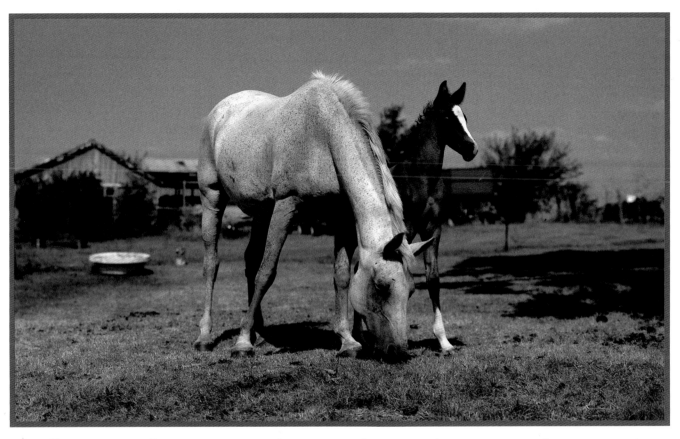

Some farmers keep horses to ride.

There are many farm animals in this book. Can you think of any others?

Wild animals

Many wild animals live on farms. Farms give them food and shelter.

▶ *Birds nest in the barns.*

Farmers shut chickens up at night to try to keep them safe from foxes.

◀ Foxes take a chicken if they can.

I know that...

1 Many animals live on farms.

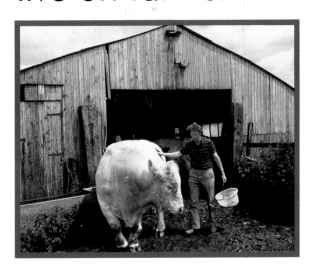

2 Farmers give animals food and shelter.

3 Cows give us milk and meat.

4 Sheep give us wool, milk and meat.

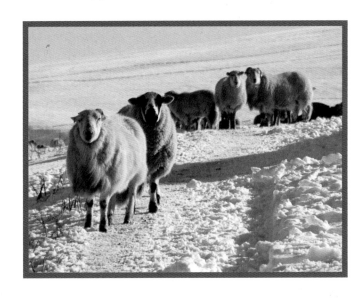

5 Chickens give us meat and eggs.

6 Pigs give us meat.

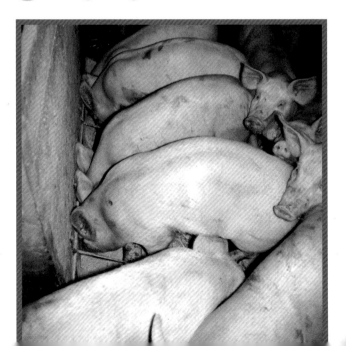

7 Cats, dogs and horses also live on farms.

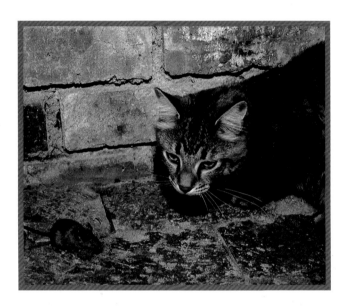

8 Some wild animals make their homes on farms.

Index

About this book

I Know That! is designed to introduce children to the process of gathering information and using reference books, one of the key skills needed to begin more formal learning at school. For this reason, each book's structure reflects the information books children will use later in their learning career – with key information in the main text and additional facts and ideas in the captions. The panels give an opportunity for further activities, ideas or discussions. The contents page and index are helpful reference guides.

The language is carefully chosen to be accessible to children just beginning to read. Illustrations support the text but also give information in their own right; active consideration and discussion of images is another key referencing skill. The main aim of the series is to build confidence - showing children how much they already know and giving them the ability to gather new information for themselves. With this in mind, the *I know that...* section at the end of the book is a simple way for children to revisit what they already know as well as what they have learnt from reading the book.